Rocks

by Adele D. Richardson

Consultant:
Francesca Pozzi, Research Associate
Center for International Earth Science Information Network
Columbia University

Bridgestone Books
an imprint of Capstone Press
Mankato, Minnesota

Bridgestone Books are published by Capstone Press,
151 Good Counsel Drive, P.O. Box 669, Mankato, Minnesota 56002.
www.capstonepress.com

Library of Congress Cataloging-in-Publication Data
Richardson, Adele, 1966–
    Rocks/by Adele D. Richardson.
    p. cm.—(The Bridgestone science library)
    Includes bibliographical references and index.
    ISBN-13: 978-0-7368-0953-5 (hardcover)   ISBN-10: 0-7368-0953-8 (hardcover)
    ISBN-13: 978-0-7368-3299-1 (softcover pbk.)   ISBN-10: 0-7368-3299-8 (softcover pbk.)
    1. Rocks—Juvenile literature. [1. Rocks.] I. Title. II. Series.
QE432.2 .R329 2002
552—dc21   00-012595

Summary: Discusses the different types of rocks, their properties, and how they form.

Editorial Credits

Erika Mikkelson, editor; Karen Risch, product planning editor; Linda Clavel, designer and
    illustrator; Jeff Anderson, photo researcher

Photo Credits

Capstone Press/Gary Sundermeyer, 8 (1–9)
Digital Wisdom, globe image
Jeff Greenberg/Photo Agora, 20
Kent and Donna Dannen, 4, 6–7 (all)
Louise K. Broman/Root Resources, 12
Mary A. Root/Root Resources, 18
Photri/C.W. Biedel, 16
Pictor, 8 (10)
Sharon Gerig/TOM STACK & ASSOCIATES, 14
Visual Unlimited/Carlyn Galati, cover, 1

Cover photo: Devil's Marbles, Tennant Creek, Northern Territory, Australia

1 2 3 4 5 6 07 06 05 04 03 02

Table of Contents

What Is a Rock? 5

Types of Rocks 6

The Mohs Scale of Hardness 9

The Rock Cycle 11

Igneous Rock 13

Sedimentary Rock 15

Layers of Rock 17

Metamorphic Rock 19

Marble 21

Hands On: Make Rock Layers 22

Words to Know 23

Read More 23

Useful Addresses 24

Internet Sites 24

Index 24

Fun Fact

Water and wind constantly change the shape of rocks in the Badlands.

What Is a Rock?

Rocks are found all over Earth. Rocks are solid, natural elements. Many minerals and other materials make up rocks. Rocks made of two or more minerals are aggregates. Rocks can be as small as pebbles or as large as a canyon wall. Some rocks are smooth. Other rocks are very rough.

Thick layers of rock make up Earth. Earth's outer layer is the crust. Hard, cool rocks cover this surface. A layer of hot liquid rock, called the mantle, is below the crust.

The outer core is below the mantle. Melted rocks form the outer core. The outer core is about 1,800 to 3,200 miles (2,900 to 5,100 kilometers) below Earth's surface.

The center of Earth is the inner core. This giant, solid ball measures about 1,500 miles (2,400 kilometers) across. Scientists believe the metals iron and nickel make up the inner core. Iron and nickel also are found in rocks on Earth's surface.

Some rocks in South Dakota's Badlands National Park formed 75 million years ago.

Types of Rocks

Scientists group rocks by how they form. The three main types of rock are igneous, sedimentary, and metamorphic.

basalt

Igneous rock forms in the mantle below Earth's surface. Heat beneath the surface melts rock. The melted rock then mixes with hot gases to form magma. Magma changes into igneous rock when it comes to the surface and cools.

Sedimentary rock has layers of matter that pressed together over time. Rocks, mud, and rotting plants and animals stack up in layers to form sedimentary rocks. Each new layer presses down on the ones below it. Over time, pressure from the top layers turns the bottom layers into rock.

sandstone, siltstone, shale, and coal

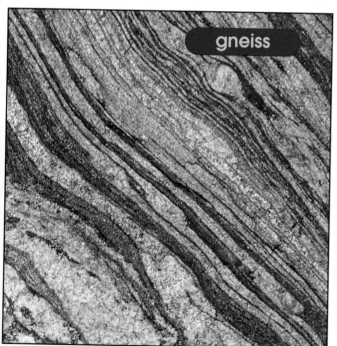

gneiss

Metamorphic rock forms from igneous or sedimentary rocks. High heat and pressure change these rocks. But often they do not melt. Instead, the heat and pressure turn igneous and sedimentary rocks into metamorphic rock.

7

The Mohs Scale of Hardness

 1. Talc

 2. Gypsum

 3. Calcite

 4. Fluorite

 5. Apatite

 6. Orthoclase

 7. Quartz

 8. Topaz

 9. Corundum

 10. Diamond

The Mohs Scale of Hardness

In 1822, scientist Freidrich Mohs created a scale of hardness. Scientists use the Mohs scale to group minerals. The Mohs scale lists 10 common minerals. The scale rates these minerals from 1 to 10. Each number stands for the hardness of a mineral. The softest mineral is a 1. The hardest mineral is a 10.

Scientists place minerals on the Mohs scale using a scratch test. Minerals that are low on the Mohs scale are more easily scratched than minerals that are higher. For example, scientists may want to test the hardness of granite. Feldspar makes up granite. Scientists could try to scratch feldspar with minerals on the scale. Feldspar would scratch orthoclase, but not quartz. Granite would fall between 6 and 7 on the Mohs scale.

Scientists also use the Mohs scale to measure the hardness of rocks. All rocks are made up of minerals. Scientists place rocks on the scale based on the minerals they contain.

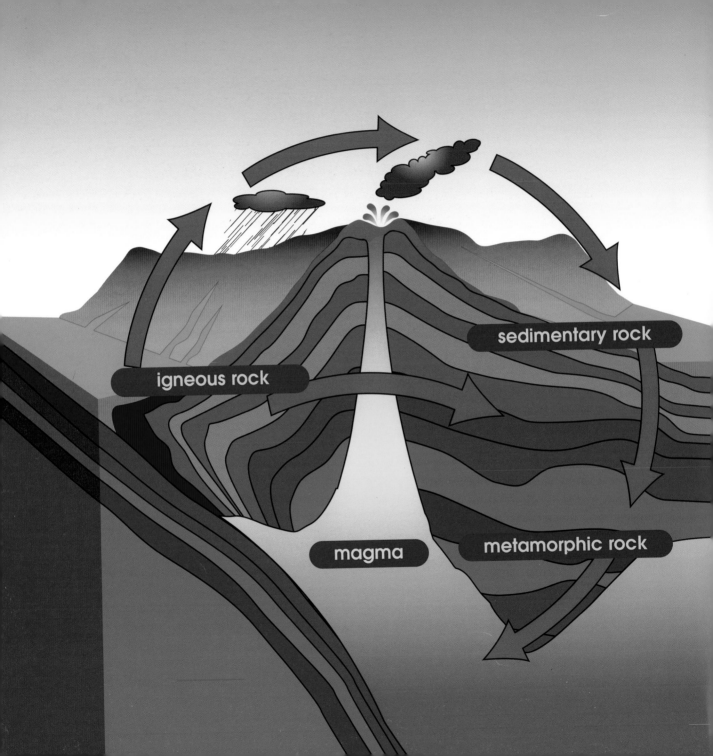

The Rock Cycle

Rocks change into different types of rocks over thousands or millions of years. Geologists call this pattern of change the rock cycle.

The rock cycle can start with igneous rock. Hot magma cools and hardens into igneous rock. Wind and rain erode igneous rock by sweeping away tiny bits of rock. Rivers and streams carry some of the rock to oceans. Layers of rock pile up on the ocean floor. The weight of the layers presses down to form sedimentary rock.

Pressure and heat from below Earth's surface change sedimentary rock. Pressure from earthquakes also changes the rock. The rock is pressed tightly together and changes into metamorphic rock.

Movements of Earth's crust can push rocks into the mantle. In the mantle, rocks melt to form magma. Magma that is pushed toward the crust cools and forms igneous rocks. Then the rock cycle continues.

Fun Fact

Extrusive rocks form outside the Earth's surface. The prefix "ex" means out of. Intrusive rocks form inside the Earth. The prefix "in" means in or into.

Igneous Rock

Cooled magma forms igneous rock. Igneous rocks that form below Earth's crust are called intrusive rocks. Igneous rocks that form on Earth's surface are called extrusive rocks.

Intrusive rocks form when hot magma fills cracks in Earth's crust. Mineral crystals form as the magma cools. Diamond and quartz are minerals that form in intrusive rock.

Extrusive rocks form when magma flows to the Earth's surface through volcanoes. The magma that flows out of volcanoes is called lava. Lava cools and hardens quickly. This process sometimes creates smooth and glassy rocks, such as black obsidian.

Basalt is the most common lava rock. A layer of basalt lies underneath the ocean floor. Islands such as Hawaii are made up of layers of basalt.

Granite is an intrusive rock.

Sedimentary Rock

Sedimentary rock forms from layers of existing rocks and rotting plants and animals. The three types of sedimentary rock are clastic rocks, chemically formed rocks, and organically formed rocks.

Layers of pebbles and sand make up clastic rocks. These rocks look like pieces of cement with pebbles stuck in them. Sandstone is clastic rock. Tiny grains of sand pressed together over time form sandstone.

Chemically formed rocks often are found in caves. Water drips from cave ceilings and leaves minerals behind. Over time, long, spearlike mineral deposits hang from a cave ceiling. They form stalactites.

Layers of rotting plants and animals make up organically formed rocks. Over time, the rotting matter turns into rock. Coal is one type of organically formed rock. Scientists often find fossils in organically formed sedimentary rock.

Over time, layers of tiny grains of quartz and feldspar are pressed together to make sandstone.

What Is a Petrologist?

A petrologist is a scientist who studies rocks. These scientists label rocks and put them into groups. To do this, petrologists look closely at the rocks. They hold a rock up to a light to look at its colors. Petrologists also notice the rock's shape. They sometimes use a microscope to discover the minerals that make up the rock.

Layers of Rock

Layers of sedimentary rock are strata. Many strata of rock can stack up over long periods of time. This process of making layers is called stratification.

Stratification occurs on land and in oceans. Wind and rain erode rocks on land. The eroded pieces then settle in low areas of land. In oceans, water currents wear away rocks. These eroded rocks then sink to the ocean floor. The top layer's weight presses on the bottom layers to form the strata seen in many sedimentary rocks.

People often can see several layers of strata in canyons. They also can see strata when roads are cut through mountains.

Scientists study strata to learn about Earth's past. They can learn about the age of the Earth by looking at the rocks that make up different strata. Scientists sometimes find fossils of plants and animals in strata. The fossils give clues about what Earth was like thousands of years ago.

Layers of rock can be many different colors.

Metamorphic Rock

Heat and pressure inside Earth's crust change the makeup and appearance of rocks. Scientists call these changed rocks metamorphic rocks. Heat and pressure can change any rock several times.

A metamorphic rock often is very different from the original rock. A rock's color, hardness, or smoothness can change.

Shale is a sedimentary rock. This soft rock can be black, gray, green, red, or yellow. With pressure, shale turns into a metamorphic rock called slate.

Slate is a harder rock than shale. It breaks up into smooth, thin pieces. Slate can be black, green, purple, or red.

With even more pressure, slate turns into a metamorphic rock called schist. Schist is a very hard, glassy rock. It can be black, gray, green, red, or white.

Slate is a metamorphic rock.

Marble

Marble is a metamorphic rock. Millions of years ago, all marble was limestone. Limestone is a sedimentary rock. Heat and pressure within Earth turned some of the limestone into marble.

Marble is a soft rock. Wind and water erode marble more quickly than other types of rock. Marble does not break or split like other rocks. Its surface becomes smooth and shiny as the top layers wear away.

Several colors of marble exist. But some types of marble are rare. Pure white and rosy pink marble are hard to find. Black, gray, and mixed color marble are more common.

Marble is found throughout the world. Most marble comes from quarries in Greece and Italy. Miners remove marble from the ground there.

Artists sometimes create sculptures from marble. They easily can cut and polish the marble into many shapes.

Some artists create sculptures from marble.

Hands On: Make Rock Layers

Sedimentary rocks form over time. Their top layers press down on lower layers. Eventually, the layers at the bottom turn into rock. You can learn how gravity helps form the layers of sedimentary rock.

What You Need

Pebbles
Dirt
Glass bowl
Water
Spoon

What You Do

1. Place the pebbles and dirt in a glass bowl.
2. Add water until the bowl is almost full.
3. Stir the contents of the bowl.
4. Let the bowl sit for 10 minutes. What happens?

The contents of the bowl settle into different layers. Gravity pulled the rocks to the bottom of the bowl. Rocks are heavier than dirt. Gravity pulls heavier materials to the bottom layers of sedimentary rocks.

Words to Know

erode (e-RODE)—to wear away; wind and water erode rock.
fossil (FOSS-uhl)—the preserved remains of a plant or animal
lava (LAH-vuh)—the hot, liquid rock that pours out of a volcano when it erupts
magma (MAG-muh)—melted rock below Earth's surface
mineral (MIN-ur-uhl)—a substance found in nature that is not made by a plant or animal; minerals can be found on Earth's surface or underground.
pressure (PRESH-ur)—the force produced by pressing on something
stalactite (stuh-LAK-tite)—a thin piece of rock that hangs from a cave ceiling

Read More

Downs, Sandra. *Earth's Hidden Treasures.* Exploring Planet Earth. Brookfield, Conn.: Twenty-First Century Books, 1999.

Flanagan, Alice K. *Rocks.* Simply Science. Minneapolis: Compass Point Books, 2001.

Gallant, Roy A. *Rocks.* Kaleidoscope. Tarrytown, N.Y.: Benchmark Books, 2000.

Useful Addresses

**American Geological
  Institute**
AGI Education Department
4220 King Street
Alexandria, VA 22302-1502

**Geological Survey of Canada
  Earth Sciences Sector**
350–601 Booth Street
Ottawa, ON K1A 0E8
Canada

Internet Sites

FactHound offers a safe, fun way to find Internet sites related to this book.
All of the sites on FactHound have been researched by our staff.

Here's how:
1. Visit www.facthound.com
2. Type in this special code 0736809538 for
   age-appropriate sites. Or enter a search word
   related to this book for a more general search.
3. Click on the Fetch It button.

FactHound will fetch the best sites for you!

Index

aggregates, 5
basalt, 13
coal, 15
igneous rock, 6, 7, 11, 13
magma, 6, 11, 13
mantle, 5, 6, 11

metamorphic rock, 6, 7, 11,
    19, 21
Mohs, Freidrich, 9
sedimentary rock, 6, 7, 11,
    15, 17, 19, 21
strata, 17